Doily Instructions

To make stunning doilies, you need only a steel crochet hook, some crochet thread and a tapestry needle. To give your doilies a more finished look, you will also need blocking and starching supplies.

Steel Hooks

If you have not worked with steel hooks and finer thread, don't be afraid to try. You will be using exactly the same stitches you are familiar with, but at first it may feel clumsy and awkward. For an experienced crocheter, this is a bit of a surprise, suddenly feeling all thumbs again just as when you first learned to crochet. But this will pass in a few hours of crocheting, as you adjust your tension and working method to the new tools. Soon you will work much more by feel than when working with heavier yarns and aluminum hooks.

Steel hooks range in size from 00 (large) to 14 (very fine), and are 5" long, which is shorter than the aluminum or plastic hooks. Their shape is different from other crochet hooks. There is the throat, then the shank, and after the shank the steel begins to widen again before it reaches the finger grip.

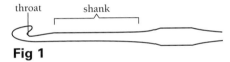

Fig 1

When crocheting, it is important that the stitches do not slide beyond the shank as this will cause a loose tension and alter the gauge. If you find you are having difficulty at first, put a piece of cellophane tape around the hook to keep the stitches from sliding past the correct area. With practice, you will work in the right place automatically.

Thread

Thread comes in many sizes: from very fine crochet cotton (sizes 80 and 100) used for lace making and tatting, to sizes 10 and 20 used for doilies, tablecloths and bedspreads. The larger the number, the thinner the thread. The most commonly used thread is size 10, and is often called bedspread weight. It is readily available in white, ecru and cream as well as a wide variety of beautiful colors. This is the weight used for the doilies in this book. Always read thread labels carefully. The label will tell you how much thread is in the ball in ounces, grams, meters or yards; the type of thread, usually cotton, and its washability. Also, there is usually a dye lot number. This number assures you that the color of each ball with this number is the same. The same color may vary from dye lot, to dye lot creating variations in color when a project is completed. Therefore, when purchasing thread for a project, it is important to match the dye lot number on the balls and purchase enough thread to complete the project.

Beginning a Doily

Besides the usual crochet stitches, which are found in our Stitch Guide on page 16, the two techniques that you need to know are how to join a chain into a circle and how to join the end of a round to the beginning of the same round.

To practice, chain 6. Insert the hook through the first chain you made (next to the slip knot, **Fig 2**).

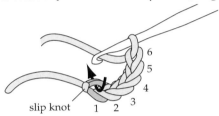

Fig 2

Hook the thread and draw it through the chain and through the loop on the hook; you have now joined the 6 chains into a circle or ring. This is the way most doilies are started.

Now, chain 3 and work 11 double crochet stitches into the center of the circle. To join the round, insert the hook in the third chain of the beginning chain 3 **(Fig 3)**, hook thread and draw it through the chain and through the loop on the hook. You have joined the round.

Fig 3

Blocking Information

Blocking means "setting" the finished doily into its final size and shape. To do this, wash the doily carefully by hand using a mild soap if necessary and rinse well in warm water. Spread the wet doily out on a flat padded surface, having the right side facing up. Smooth the doily out to the correct size, having the design properly aligned with all picots, loops, etc., open. If necessary, use rustproof pins to hold edges in place. Let dry thoroughly before removing.

Starching Information

If you want your doily to have a stiffer shape, it will be necessary to starch the doily before blocking it. To do this, you will need the following supplies:

1. A commercial stiffening solution or white craft glue thoroughly mixed with an equal amount of water.

2. A plastic bag that locks across the top for soaking the doily.

3. A sheet of Styrofoam brand (our preference) or a piece of corrugated cardboard to use as a pinning board.

4. Plastic wrap to cover pinning board so doily can be easily removed.

After assembling the supplies, wash doily as described under Blocking Information. Pour prepared stiffening solution into plastic bag. Immerse doily in solution and let soak one minute. Remove and press out excess solution. Do not squeeze—doily should be very wet, but there should be no solution in the decorative holes (dab with a dry paper towel to correct this).

Place doily on covered pinning board and pin as described under Blocking.

Lacy Bouquet Doily

EASY

Size:
11" diameter

Materials:
Bedspread weight crochet cotton, 175 yds ecru

Size 7 (1.65mm) steel crochet hook, or size required for gauge

Size 16 tapestry needle

Gauge:
Rnds 1 through 4 = 2¼"

Instructions
Ch 5, join to form a ring.

Rnd 1 (right side):
Ch 5 (counts as a dc and a ch-2 sp), (dc in ring, ch 2) 7 times; join in 3rd ch of beg ch-5—8 ch-2 sps.

Rnd 2:
Sl st in next ch-2 sp, ch 3 (counts as a dc on this and following rnds), 2 dc in same sp; ch 1; * 3 dc in next ch-2 sp; ch 1; rep; from * 6 times more; join in 3rd ch of beg ch-3.

Rnd 3:
Ch 3, dc in next 2 dc, ch 4, sk next ch-1 sp; * dc in next 3 dc, ch 4, sk next ch-1 sp; rep from * 6 times more; join in 3rd ch of beg ch-3.

Rnd 4:
Sl st in next 2 dc and in next ch-4 sp, ch 3, in same sp work (dc, ch 3, 2 dc); ch 5, sk next 3 dc; * in next ch-4 sp work (2 dc, ch 3, 2 dc); ch 5, sk next 3 dc; rep from * 6 times more; join in 3rd ch of beg ch-3.

Rnd 5:
Sl st in next dc and in next ch-3 sp, ch 3, in same sp work (2 dc, ch 3, 3 dc)—beg shell made; ch 5, sk next ch-5 sp; * in next ch-3 sp work (3 dc, ch 3, 3 dc)—shell made; ch 5, sk next ch-5 sp; rep from * 6 times more; join in 3rd ch of beg ch-3.

Rnd 6:
Sl st in next 2 dc and in next ch-3 sp; beg shell in same sp; * † ch 5, working over next ch-5 sp, sc in corresponding ch-5 sp on 2nd rnd below; ch 5 †; shell in ch-3 sp of next shell—shell in shell made; rep from * 6 times more, then rep from † to † once; join in 3rd ch of beg ch-3.

Rnd 7:
Sl st in next 2 dc and in next ch-3 sp; beg shell in same sp; * † ch 3, sc next ch-5 sp, ch 5, sc in next ch-5 sp, ch 3 †; shell in next shell; rep from * 6 times more, then rep from † to † once; join in 3rd ch of beg ch-3.

Rnd 8:
Sl st in next 2 dc and in next ch-3 sp; beg shell in same sp; * † ch 5, sk next ch-3 sp, in next ch-5 sp work (2 trc, ch 3, 2 trc); ch 5, sk next ch-3 sp †; shell in next shell; rep from * 6 times more, then rep from † to † once; join in 3rd ch of beg ch-3.

Rnd 9:
Sl st in next 2 dc and in next ch-3 sp; beg shell in same sp; * † ch 5, sk next ch-5 sp, shell in next ch-3 sp; ch 5, sk next ch-5 sp †; shell in next shell; rep

from * 6 times more, then rep from † to † once; join in 3rd ch of beg ch-3.

Rnd 10:
Sl st in next 2 dc and in next ch-3 sp; beg shell in same sp; * † ch 4, sl st in 4th ch from hook—picot made; ch 4, working over next ch-5 lp, sc in corresponding ch-5 lp on 2nd rnd below; ch 8, sl st in 4th ch from hook—picot made †; shell in next shell; rep from * 14 times more, then rep from † to † once; join in 3rd ch of beg ch-3.

Rnd 11:
Sl st in next 2 dc and in next ch-3 sp; ch 1, sc in same sp; * † ch 4, sc in next picot, ch 4, sk next 2 ch-4 sps, sc in next picot, ch 4 †; sc in ch-3 sp of next shell; rep from * 14 times more, then rep from † to † once; join in first sc.

Rnd 12:
Ch 3, 3 dc in next ch-4 sp; * dc in next sc, 3 dc in next ch-4 sp; rep from * around; join in 3rd ch of beg ch-3.

Rnd 13:
Sl st in next dc, ch 3, dc in next 6 dc, ch 3, sk next dc; * dc in next 7 dc, ch 3, sk next dc; rep from * around; join in 3rd ch of beg ch-3.

Rnd 14:
Sl st in next 6 dc and in next ch-3 sp; ch 7 (counts as a trc and a ch-3 sp), trc in same sp; * ch 4, sk next 3 dc, sc in next dc, ch 4, sk next 3 dc, in next ch-3 sp work (trc, ch 3, trc); rep from * 22 times more; ch 4, sk next 3 sl sts, sc in next sl st, ch 4, sk next 3 sl sts; join in 4th ch of beg ch-7.

Rnd 15:
Sl st in next ch-3 sp, ch 3, in same sp work (dc, ch 3, 2 dc); * ch 7, sk next 2 ch-4 sps, in next ch-3 sp work (2 dc, ch 3, 2 dc); rep from * 22 times more; ch 7, sk next 2 ch-4 sps; join in 3rd ch of beg ch-3.

Rnd 16:
Sl st in next dc and in next ch-3 sp; beg shell in same sp; * ch 7, sk next ch-7 sp, shell in next ch-3 sp; rep from * 22 times more; ch 7, sk next ch-7 sp; join in 3rd ch of beg ch-3.

Rnd 17:
Sl st in next 2 dc and in next ch-3 sp; beg shell in

same sp; * ch 8, s[...] rep from * to last [...] in 3rd ch of beg c[...]

Rnd 18:
Sl st in next 2 dc and in next ch-3 sp; ch 6, hdc in 3rd ch from hook—picot made; dc in same sp; † ch 3, hdc in top of dc just made—picot made; dc in same sp †; rep from † to † twice more; * †† ch 6, working over next ch-8 lp and corresponding ch-8 lp on prev rnd, sc in corresponding ch-7 lp on 3rd rnd below; ch 6 ††; dc in ch-3 sp of next shell; rep from † to † 4 times; rep from * 22 times more, then rep from †† to †† once; join in 3rd ch of beg ch-6 (next to picot).
Finish off and weave in ends.

Simplicity Lace Doily

EASY

Size:
11½" diameter

Materials:
Bedspread weight crochet cotton, 250 yds white

Size 7 (1.65mm) steel crochet hook, or size required for gauge

Size 16 tapestry needle

Gauge:
Rnds 1 through 7 = 5"

Pattern Stitch:

Cluster (CL):
Keeping last lp of each trc on hook, trc in 2 sps indicated; YO and draw through all 3 lps on hook—CL made.

Instructions
Ch 8, join to form a ring.

Rnd 1 (right side):
Ch 3 (counts as a dc), 23 dc in ring; join in 3rd ch of beg ch-3—24 dc.

Rnd 2:
Ch 6 (counts as a dc and a ch-3 sp), dc in next dc, ch 1; * dc in next dc, ch 3, dc in next dc, ch 1; rep from * 10 times more; join in 3rd ch of beg ch-6.

Rnd 3:
Sl st in next ch-3 sp; ch 9 (counts as a dc and a ch-6 sp), sk next ch-1 sp, dc in next ch-3 sp; * ch 6, sk next ch-1 sp, dc in next ch-3 sp; rep from * 9 times more; ch 3, sk next ch-1 sp; join with a dc in 3rd ch of beg ch-9.

Rnd 4:
Ch 3, trc in next ch-6 sp; * ch 8, CL (see Pattern Stitch) over same ch-6 sp and next ch-6 sp; rep from * 9 times more; ch 8, CL over same ch-6 sp and sp formed by ch-3 and joining dc of prev rnd; ch 8, sk beg ch-3; join in first trc—12 ch-8 sps.

Rnd 5:
Ch 7 (counts as a trc and a ch-3 sp), trc in same trc as joining; * ch 3, sc in next ch-8 sp, ch 3, in next CL work (trc, ch 3, trc); rep from * 10 times more; ch 3, sc in next ch-8 sp; ch 3; join in 4th ch of beg ch-7.

Rnd 6:
Ch 1, sc in next ch-3 sp; * ch 11, sk next 2 ch-3 sps, sc in next ch-3 sp; rep from * 10 times more; ch 11, sk next 2 ch-3 sps; join in first sc.

Rnd 7:
Ch 1, sk first ch of next ch-11 sp, sl st in next ch; ch 5 (counts as a trc and a ch-1 sp on this and following

rnds), trc in next ch, (ch 1, trc in next ch) 7 times;
* sk next ch, next sc, and first ch of next ch-11 sp; trc in next ch, (ch 1, trc in next ch) 8 times; rep from
* 10 times more; sk next ch; join in 4th ch of beg ch-5.

Rnd 8:
SI st in next trc and in next ch-1 sp, ch 1, sc in next trc; * ch 7, sk next 3 trc, sc in next trc, ch 7, sk next 4 trc, sc in next trc; rep from * 10 times more; ch 7, sk next 3 trc, sc in next trc, ch 3; join with a trc in first sc.

Rnd 9:
Ch 5, in top of joining trc work (trc, ch 1) 3 times; trc in same st; * ch 7, sc in next ch-7 sp, ch 7, sk next 3 chs of next ch-7 sp, in next ch work (trc, ch 1) 4 times; trc in same ch; rep from * 10 times more; ch 7, sc in next ch-7 sp, ch 3; join with a trc in 4th ch of beg ch-5.

Rnd 10:
Ch 7, sk beg ch-5 and next trc, sc in next trc; * (ch 7, sc in next ch-7 sp) twice; ch 7, sk next 2 trc, sc in next trc; rep from * 10 times more; ch 7, sc in next ch-7 sp, ch 3; join with a trc in top of joining trc of prev rnd.

Rnd 11:
Ch 5, in top of joining trc work (trc, ch 1) 3 times; trc in same st; * † ch 3, sc in next ch-7 sp, ch 3, in next sc work (trc, ch 1) twice; trc in same sc; ch 3, sc in next ch-7 sp, ch 3 †; sk next 3 chs of next ch-7 sp, in next ch work (trc, ch 1) 4 times; trc in same ch; rep from * 10 times more, then rep from † to † once; join in 4th ch of beg ch-5.

Rnd 12:
Ch 1, sl st in next ch-1 sp, in next trc, in next ch-1 sp, and in next trc; ch 7 (counts as a trc and a ch-3 sp), trc in same trc as last sl st made; * † ch 3, CL over next 2 ch-3 sps; ch 3, sk next trc, in next trc work

(trc, ch 3, trc); ch 3, CL over next 2 ch-3 sps; ch 3 †; sk next 2 trc, in next trc work (trc, ch 3, trc); rep from * 10 times more, then rep from † to † once; join in 4th ch of beg ch-7.

Rnd 13:
Ch 1, sc in next ch-1 sp; ch 4, sk next ch-3 sp, in next CL work (trc, ch 3, trc); ch 4; * sk next ch-3 sp, sc in next ch-3 sp, ch 4, sk next ch-3 sp, in next CL work (trc, ch 3, trc); ch 4; rep from * around; join in first sc.

Rnd 14:
SI st in next 4 chs and in next trc; ch 1; * sc in next ch-3 sp, ch 13, sk next 2 ch-4 sps; rep from * around; join in first sc—24 ch-13 sps.

Rnd 15:
SI st in next 3 chs of next ch-13 sp, ch 5, trc in next ch, (ch 1, trc in next ch) 7 times; sk next 2 chs of same ch-13 sp, next sc, and next 2 chs on next ch-13 sp; * trc in next ch, (ch 1, trc in next ch) 8 times; sk next 2 chs of same ch-13 sp, next sc, and next 2 chs on next ch-13 sp; rep from * around; join in 4th ch of beg ch-5.

Rnd 16:
SI st in next trc and in next ch-1 sp, ch 1, sc in next trc; * ch 7, sk next 3 trc, sc in next trc, ch 7, sk next 4 trc, sc in next trc; rep from * 22 times more; ch 7, sk next 3 trc, sc in next trc, ch 3, sk next 2 trc; join with a trc in first sc.

Rnd 17:
Ch 5, in top of joining trc work (trc, ch 1) 3 times; trc in same st; ch 4, sc in 4th ch of next ch-7 sp, ch 4; * in 4th ch of next ch-7 sp work (trc, ch 1) 4 times; trc in same ch; ch 4; rep from * around; join in 4th ch of beg ch-5.
Finish off and weave in ends.

Pinwheel Doily

EASY

Size:
13" diameter

Materials:
Bedspread weight crochet cotton, 200 yds cream
Size 7 (1.65mm) steel crochet hook, or size required for gauge
Size 16 tapestry needle

Gauge:
Rnds 1 through 6 = 3¼"

Instructions
Ch 7, join to form a ring.

Rnd 1 (right side):
Ch 5 (counts as a dc and a ch-2 sp), (dc in ring, ch 2) 8 times; join in 3rd ch of beg ch-5—9 ch-2 sps.

Rnd 2:
Ch 3 (counts as a dc on this and following rnds), dc in same ch as joining; ch 3, sk next ch-2 sp; * 2 dc in next dc; ch 3, sk next ch-2 sp; rep from * 7 times more; join in 3rd ch of beg ch-3.

Rnd 3:
Sl st in next dc and in next ch-3 sp; ch 1, sc in same sp; ch 7; * sc in next ch-3 sp, ch 7; rep from * 8 times more; join in first sc.

Rnd 4:
Sl st in next ch-7 sp, ch 3 (counts as a dc on this and following rnds), 4 dc in same sp; ch 3; * 5 dc in next ch-7 sp, ch 3; rep from * 7 times more; join in 3rd ch of beg ch-3.

Rnd 5:
Ch 3, dc in next 2 dc; * † ch 3, sk next 2 dc, 4 dc in next ch-3 sp †; dc in next 3 dc; rep from * 7 times more, then rep from † to † once; join in 3rd ch of beg ch-3.

Rnd 6:
Ch 6 (counts as a dc and a ch-3 sp); * 4 dc in next ch-3 sp; dc in next 5 dc, ch 3, sk next 2 dc; rep from * 7 times more; 4 dc in ch-3 sp; dc in next 4 dc; join in 3rd ch of beg ch-6.

Rnd 7:
Sl st in next ch-3 sp, ch 3, 3 dc in same sp; * dc in next 7 dc, ch 3, sk next 2 dc, 4 dc in next ch-3 sp; rep from * 7 times more; dc in next 7 dc, ch 3; join in 3rd ch of beg ch-3.

Rnd 8:
Ch 3, dc in next 8 dc; * † ch 3, sk next 2 dc, 4 dc in next ch-3 sp †; dc in next 9 dc; rep from * 7 times more, then rep from † to † once; join in 3rd of beg ch-3.

Rnd 9:
Ch 3, dc in next 6 dc; * † ch 3, sk next 2 dc, 4 dc in next ch-3 sp †; dc in next 11 dc; rep from * 7 times more, then rep from † to † once; dc in next 4 dc; join in 3rd ch of beg ch-3.

Rnd 10:
Ch 3, dc in next 4 dc; * † ch 3, sk next 2 dc, dc in next ch-3 sp, ch 3 †; dc in next 13 dc; rep from * 7 times more, then rep from † to † once; dc in next 8 dc; join in 3rd ch of beg ch-3. Finish off.

Rnd 11:
Join in first dc of any 13-dc group; ch 3, dc in next 10 dc; * † ch 4, sk next 2 dc, sc in next ch-3 sp (work sc at end of sp), in next dc, and in next ch-3 sp (work sc at beg of sp); ch 4 †; dc in next 11 dc; rep from * 7 times more, then rep from † to † once; join in 3rd ch of beg ch-3.

Rnd 12:
Ch 3, dc in next 8 dc; * † ch 6, sk next 2 dc and next ch-4 sp, dc in next 3 sc, ch 6 †; sk next ch-4 sp, dc in next 9 dc; rep from * 7 times more, then rep from † to † once; join in 3rd ch of beg ch-3.

Rnd 13:
Ch 3, dc in next 6 dc; * † ch 5, sk next 2 dc, dc in next ch-6 sp, ch 5, sk next dc, sc in next dc, ch 5, dc in next ch-6 sp, ch 5 †; dc in next 7 dc; rep from * 7 times more, then rep from † to † once; join in 3rd ch of beg ch-3.

Rnd 14:
Ch 3, dc in next 4 dc; * † ch 5, sk next 2 dc, sc in next ch-5 sp (work sc at end of sp), in next dc, and in next ch-5 sp (work sc at beg of sp); ch 6, sk next sc, sc in next ch-5 sp (work sc at end of sp), in next dc, and in next ch-5 sp (work sc at beg of sp); ch 5 †; dc in next 5 dc; rep from * 7 times more, then rep from † to † once; join in 3rd ch of beg ch-3.

Rnd 15:
Ch 3, dc in next 2 dc; * † ch 6, sk next 2 dc and next ch-5 sp, dc in next 3 sc, ch 5, sc in next ch-6 sp, ch 5, dc in next 3 sc, ch 6 †; sk next ch-5 sp, dc in next 3 dc; rep from * 7 times more, then rep from † to † once; join in 3rd ch of beg ch-3.

Rnd 16:
Ch 2, dc in next dc; * † ch 5, sk next dc, dc in next ch-6 sp, ch 5, sk next dc, sc in next dc, (ch 5, sc in next ch-5 sp) twice; ch 5, sk next dc, sc in next dc, ch 5, dc in next ch-6 sp †; ch 5, dec over next 2 dc [to work dec: (YO, draw up lp in next dc, YO and draw through 2 lps on hook) twice; YO and draw through all 3 lps on hook—dec made]; rep from * 7 times more, then rep from † to † once; ch 2, sk beg ch-2; join with a dc in first dc.

Rnd 17:
Ch 6; * sc in next ch-5 sp, ch 6; rep from * to last ch-5 sp; sc in last ch-5 sp, ch 3; join with a dc in top of joining dc of prev rnd.

Rnd 18:
Ch 6; * sc in next ch-6 sp, ch 6; rep from * to last ch-6 sp; sc in last ch-6 sp, ch 3; join with a dc in top of joining dc of prev rnd.

Rnd 19:
Rep Rnd 18.

Rnd 20:
Ch 6; * sc in next ch-6 sp, ch 6; rep from * around; join with an sc in top of joining dc of prev rnd.

Rnd 21:
Sl st in next ch-6 sp, ch 3, 2 dc in same lp; ch 3, 3 dc in next ch-6 sp; ch 3; rep from * around; join in 3rd ch of beg ch-3.

Rnd 22:
Ch 1, sc in same ch as joining and in next 2 dc, ch 4, sk next ch-3 sp; * sc in next 3 dc, ch 4, sk next ch-3 sp; rep from * around; join in first sc.

Rnd 23:
Ch 1; * sc in next sc, ch 3, 3 dc in next ch-4 sp; ch 3, sk next sc; rep from * around; join in first sc.

Rnd 24:
Sl st in next 3 chs, ch 1; * sc in next 3 dc, ch 6, sk next 2 ch-3 sps; rep from * around; join in first sc.

Rnd 25:
Ch 1; * sc in next sc, ch 5, keeping last lp of each dc on hook, 2 dc in next ch-6 sp; YO and draw through all 3 lps on hook—cluster made; ch 3, sl st in top of cluster just made—picot made; ch 5, sk next sc; rep from * around; join in first sc.
Finish off and weave in ends.

Floral Center Doily

EASY

Size:
8½" diameter

Materials:
Bedspread weight crochet cotton, 150 yds white
Size 7 (1.65mm) steel crochet hook, or size required for gauge
Size 16 tapestry needle

Gauge:
Rnds 1 through 5 = 2¼"

Instructions
Ch 5, join to form a ring.

Rnd 1 (right side):
Ch 5 (counts as a dc and a ch-2 sp), (dc in ring, ch 2) 7 times; join in 3rd ch of beg ch-5—8 ch-2 sps.

Rnd 2:
Sl st in next ch-2 sp, ch 1, 3 sc in same sp; ch 1; * 3 sc in next ch-2 sp; ch 1; rep from * 6 times more; join in first sc.

Rnd 3:
Sl st in next 2 sc and in next ch-1 sp; ch 3 (counts as a dc on this and following rnds), 2 dc in same sp; ch 3, sk next 3 sc; * 3 dc in next ch-1 sp; ch 3, sk next 3 sc; rep from * 6 times more; join in 3rd ch of beg ch-3.

Rnd 4:
Ch 1, sc in same ch as joining and in next 2 dc; 3 sc in next ch-3 sp; * sc in next 3 dc, 3 sc in next ch-3 sp; rep from * 6 times more; join in first sc.

Rnd 5:
Sl st in next sc, ch 6 (counts as a dc and a ch-3 sp), dc in same sc; * sk next 2 sc, in next sc work (dc, ch 3, dc); rep from * 14 times more; join in 3rd ch of beg ch-6—16 ch-3 sps.

Rnd 6:
Sl st in next ch-3 sp, ch 3, 4 dc in same sp; * 5 dc in each rem ch-3 sp; join in 3rd ch of beg ch-3.

Rnd 7:
Ch 3, dc in next 4 dc, ch 1; * dc in next 5 dc, ch 1; rep from * around; join in 3rd ch of beg ch-3.

Rnd 8:
Ch 3, dc in next 4 dc, ch 2, sk next ch-1 sp; * dc in next 5 dc, ch 2, sk next ch-1 sp; rep from * around; join in 3rd ch of beg ch-3.

Rnd 9:
Ch 3, dc in next 4 dc, ch 3, sk next ch-2 sp; * dc in next 5 dc, ch 3, sk next ch-2 sp; rep from * around; join in 3rd ch of beg ch-3.

Rnd 10:
Ch 3, dc in next 4 dc, ch 4, sk next ch-3 sp; * dc in next 5 dc, ch 4, sk next ch-3 sp; rep from * around; join in 3rd ch of beg ch-3.

Rnd 11:
Ch 3, dc in next 4 dc, ch 3, dc in next ch-4 sp, ch 3; * dc in next 5 dc, ch 3, dc in next ch-4 sp, ch 3; rep from * around; join in 3rd ch of beg ch-3.

Rnd 12:
Ch 3, dc in next 4 dc, (ch 2, dc in next ch-3 sp) twice; ch 2; * dc in next 5 dc, (ch 2, dc in next ch-3 sp) twice; ch 2; rep from * around; join in 3rd ch of beg ch-3.

Rnd 13:
Sl st in next dc, ch 3, dc in next 2 dc; * † ch 2, sk next dc, dc in next ch-2 sp, (ch 2, dc in next ch-2 sp) twice; ch 2 †; sk next dc, dc in next 3 dc; rep from * 14 times more, then rep from † to † once; join in 3rd ch of beg ch-3.

Rnd 14:
Sl st in next dc, ch 5 (counts as a dc and a ch-2 sp), dc in next ch-2 sp, (ch 2, dc in next ch-2 sp) 3 times; * ch 2, sk next dc, dc in next dc, ch 2, (dc in next ch-2 sp, ch 2) 4 times; rep from * around; join in 3rd ch of beg ch-5.

Rnd 15:
Sl st in next ch-2 sp, ch 6 (counts as a dc and a ch-3 sp); * dc in next ch-2 sp, ch 3; rep from * around; join in 3rd ch of beg ch-6.

Rnd 16:
Ch 3; * † (2 dc in next ch-3 sp, dc in next dc) twice; †† ch 3, sk next ch-3 sp, dc in next dc, 2 dc in next ch-3 sp; dc in next dc ††; rep from †† to †† twice more; 2 dc in next ch-3 sp; dc in next dc, ch 3 †; sk next ch-3 sp, dc in next dc; rep from * 4 times more, then rep from † to † once; join in 3rd ch of beg ch-3.

Rnd 17:
Sl st in next 2 dc, ch 1; * sc in next dc, ch 3, sk next 3 dc, keeping last lp of each dc on hook, 2 dc in next ch-3 sp; YO and draw through all 3 lps on hook—cluster made; ch 3, in same sp work cluster; † ch 4, sk next 4 dc, in next ch-3 sp work (cluster, ch 3, cluster) †; rep from † to † once more; ch 3, sk next 3 dc, sc in next dc, ch 3, sk next 3 dc, in next ch-3 sp work (cluster, ch 3, cluster); ch 3, sk next 3 dc; rep from * around; join in first sc.
Finish off and weave in ends.

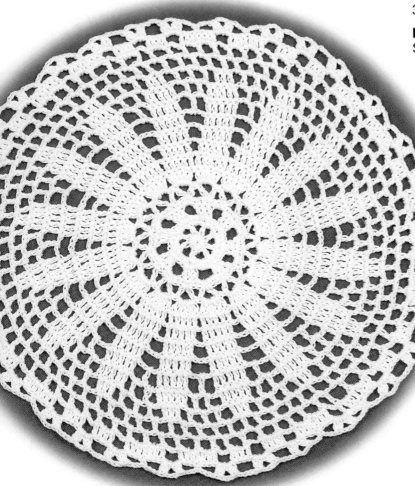

Pineapple Fantasy Doily

INTERMEDIATE

Size:
20" diameter

Materials:
Bedspread weight crochet cotton, 450 yds white
Size 7 (1.65mm) steel crochet hook, or size required for gauge
Size 16 tapestry needle

Gauge:
8 trc = 1"

Instructions
Ch 8, join to form a ring.

Rnd 1 (right side):
Ch 4 (counts as a trc on this and following rnds), 23 trc in ring; join in 4th ch of beg ch-4—24 trc.

Rnd 2:
Ch 4, 2 trc in same ch; * ch 2, sk next trc, 3 trc in next trc; rep from * 10 times more; ch 2, sk next trc; join in 4th ch of beg ch-4.

Rnd 3:
Sl st in next trc, ch 4, in same trc work (trc, ch 3, 2 trc); * ch 1, sk next ch-2 sp and next trc, in next trc work (2 trc, ch 3, 2 trc); rep from * 10 times more; ch 1, sk next ch-2 sp; join in 4th ch of beg ch-4.

Rnd 4:
Sl st in next trc and in next ch-3 sp; ch 7 (counts as a trc and a ch-3 sp), in same sp work (trc, ch 3, trc); ch 3, sk next ch-1 sp; * in next ch-3 sp work (trc, ch 3) twice; trc in same sp; ch 3, sk next ch-1 sp; rep from * 10 times more; join in 4th ch of beg ch-7.

Rnd 5:
Sl st in next sp and in next trc, ch 4, in same trc work (2 trc, ch 3, 3 trc)—beg shell made; * † ch 3, sk next ch-3 sp, sc in next ch-3 sp, ch 3 †; sk next ch-3 sp, in next trc work (3 trc, ch 3, 3 trc)—shell made; rep from * 10 times more, then rep from † to † once; join in 4th ch of beg ch-4—12 shells.

Rnd 6:
Sl st in next 2 trc and in next ch-3 sp, ch 1, sc in same sp; * † ch 6, sk next ch-3 sp, trc in next sc, ch 6, sk next ch-3 sp †; sc in ch-3 sp of next shell; rep from * 10 times more, then rep from † to † once; join in first sc.

Rnd 7:
Ch 1, sc in same sc; * † ch 4, sk next ch-6 sp, in next trc work shell; ch 4, sk next ch-6 sp †; sc in next sc; rep from * 10 times more, then rep from † to † once; join in first sc.

Rnd 8:
Ch 12 (counts as a trc and a ch-8 sp), sk next ch-4 sp, sc in ch-3 sp of next shell; * ch 8, sk next ch-4 sp, trc in next sc, ch 8, sk next ch-4 sp, sc in ch-3 sp of next shell; rep from * 10 times more; ch 8, sk next ch-4 sp; join in 4th ch of beg ch-12.

Rnd 9:
Ch 4, beg shell in same ch as joining; * † ch 6, sk next ch-8 sp, trc in next sc, ch 4, sl st in top of trc just made—picot made; ch 6, sk next ch-8 sp †; shell in next trc; rep from * 10 times more, then rep from † to † once; join in 4th ch of beg ch-4.

Rnd 10:
Sl st in next 2 trc and in next ch-3 sp; beg shell in same sp; * † ch 4, sk next ch-6 sp, 6 trc in next picot—base of pineapple made; ch 4, sk next ch-6 sp †; in ch-3 sp of next shell work shell—shell in shell made; rep from * 10 times more, then rep from † to † once; join in 4th ch of beg ch-4.

Rnd 11:
Sl st in next 2 trc and in next ch-3 sp; beg shell in same sp; * † ch 4, sk next ch-4 sp, sc in next trc, (ch 4, sc in next trc) 5 times; ch 4, sk next ch-4 sp †; shell in next shell; rep from * 10 times more, then rep from † to † once; join in 4th ch of beg ch-4.

Rnd 12:
Sl st in next 2 trc and in next ch-3 sp; beg shell in same sp; * † ch 4, sk next ch-4 sp, sc in next ch-4 sp, (ch 4, sc in next ch-4 sp) 4 times; ch 4, sk next ch-4 sp †; shell in next shell; rep from * 10 times more, then rep from † to † once; join in 4th ch of beg ch-4.

Rnd 13:
Sl st in next 2 trc and in next ch-3 sp; beg shell in same sp; * † ch 5, sk next ch-4 sp, sc in next ch-4 sp, (ch 4, sc in next ch-4 sp) 3 times; ch 5, sk next ch-4 sp †; shell in next shell; rep from * 10 times more, then rep from † to † once; join in 4th ch of beg ch-4.

Rnd 14:
Sl st in next 2 trc and in next ch-3 sp; beg shell in same sp; ch 3, 3 trc in same sp—beg double shell made; * † ch 6, sk next ch-5 sp, sc in next ch-4 sp, (ch 4, sc in next ch-4 sp) twice; ch 6, sk next ch-5 sp †; shell in next shell; ch 3, 3 trc in same sp—double shell made; rep from * 10 times more, then rep from † to † once; join in 4th ch of beg ch-4.

Rnd 15:
Sl st in next 2 trc and in next ch-3 sp; beg shell in same sp; * † ch 8, sl st in 5th ch from hook—picot

made; ch 3, shell in next ch-3 sp; ch 6, sk next ch-6 sp, sc in next ch-4 sp, ch 4, sc in next ch-4 sp, ch 6, sk next ch-6 sp †; shell in next ch-3 sp; rep from * 10 times more, then rep from † to † once; join in 4th ch of beg ch-4.

Rnd 16:
Sl st in next 2 trc and in next ch-3 sp, beg shell in same sp; * † ch 4, 7 trc in next picot—base of pineapple made; ch 4, shell in next shell; ch 6, sk next ch-6 sp, sc in next ch-4 sp, ch 6, sk next ch-6 sp †; shell in next shell; rep from * 10 times more, then rep from † to † once; join in 4th ch of beg ch-4.

Rnd 17:
Sl st in next 2 trc and in next ch-3 sp, beg shell in same sp; * † ch 4, sk next ch-4 sp, sc in next trc, (ch 4, sc in next trc) 6 times; ch 4, sk next ch-4 sp, shell in next shell; ch 6, sk next ch-6 sp, sc in next sc, ch 6, sk next ch-6 sp †; shell in next shell; rep from * 10 times more, then rep from † to † once; join in 4th ch of beg ch-4.

Rnd 18:
Sl st in next 2 trc and in next ch-3 sp, beg shell in same sp; * † ch 5, sk next ch-4 sp, sc in next ch-4 sp, (ch 4, sc in next ch-4 sp) 5 times; ch 5, sk next ch-4 sp, shell in next shell; sk next 2 ch-6 sps †; shell in next shell; rep from * 10 times more, then rep from † to † once; join in 4th ch of beg ch-4.

Rnd 19:
Sl st in next 2 trc and in next ch-3 sp, beg shell in same sp; * † ch 5, sk next ch-5 sp, sc in next ch-4 sp, (ch 4, sc in next ch-4 sp) 4 times; ch 5, sk next ch-5 sp, shell in next shell; ch 1 †; shell in next shell; rep from * 10 times more, then rep from † to † once; join in 4th ch of beg ch-4.

Rnd 20:
Sl st in next 2 trc and in next ch-3 sp, beg shell in same sp; * † ch 5, sk next ch-5 sp, sc in next ch-4 sp, (ch 4, sc in next ch-4 sp) 3 times; ch 5, sk next ch-5 sp, shell in next shell; ch 8, sl st in 5th ch from hook—picot made; ch 3 †; shell in next shell; rep from * 10 times more, then rep from † to † once; join in 4th ch of beg ch-4.

Rnd 21:
Sl st in next 2 trc and in next ch-3 sp, beg shell in same sp; * ch 5, sk next ch-5 sp, sc in next ch-4 sp, (ch 4, sc in next ch-4 sp) twice; ch 5, sk next ch-5 sp, shell in next shell; ch 3, 7 trc in next picot—

base of pineapple made; ch 3 †; shell in next shell; rep from * 10 times more, then rep from † to † once; join in 4th ch of beg ch-4.

Rnd 22:
Sl st in next 2 trc and in next ch-3 sp, beg shell in same sp; * † ch 5, sk next ch-5 sp, sc in next ch-4 sp, ch 4, sc in next ch-4 sp, ch 5, sk next ch-5 sp, shell in next shell; ch 3, sk next ch-3 sp, 2 trc in each of next 7 trc; ch 3, sk next ch-3 sp †; shell in next shell; rep from * 10 times more, then rep from † to † once; join in 4th ch of beg ch-4.

Rnd 23:
Sl st in next 2 trc and in next ch-3 sp, beg shell in same sp; * † ch 5, sk next ch-5 sp, sc in next ch-4 sp, ch 5, sk next ch-5 sp, shell in next shell; ch 3, sk next ch-3 sp, trc in next trc, (ch 1, trc in next trc) 13 times; ch 3, sk next ch-3 sp †; shell in next shell; rep from * 10 times more, then rep from † to † once; join in 4th ch of beg ch-4.

Rnd 24:
Sl st in next 2 trc and in next ch-3 sp, beg shell in same sp; * † ch 5, sk next ch-5 sp, sc in next sc, ch 5, sk next ch-5 sp, shell in next shell; ch 3, sk next ch-3 sp, trc in next trc, (ch 2, trc in next trc) 13 times; ch 3, sk next ch-3 sp †; shell in next shell; rep from * 10 times more, then rep from † to † once; join in 4th ch of beg ch-4.

Rnd 25:
Sl st in next 2 trc and in next ch-3 sp, beg shell in same sp; * † sk next 2 ch-5 sps, shell in next shell; ch 3, sk next ch-3 sp, trc in next trc, (ch 2, trc in next trc) 13 times; ch 3, sk next ch-3 sp †; shell in next shell; rep from * 10 times more, then rep from † to † once; join in 4th ch of beg ch-4.

Rnd 26:
Sl st in next 2 trc and in next ch-3 sp, ch 3, 2 dc in same sp; * † ch 4, sl st in top of dc just made—picot made; 3 dc in next ch-3 sp; ch 5, sk next ch-3 sp, sc in next ch-2 sp, (ch 6, sl st in 4th ch from hook—picot made; ch 2, sc in next ch-2 sp) 12 times; ch 5, sk next ch-3 sp †; 3 dc in next ch-3 sp; rep from * 10 times more, then rep from † to † once; join in 3rd ch of beg ch-3.
Finish off and weave in ends.

Parisian Pineapple Doily

INTERMEDIATE

Size:
15" diameter

Materials:
Bedspread weight crochet cotton, 300 yds ecru
Size 7 (1.65mm) steel crochet hook, or size required for gauge
Size 16 tapestry needle

Gauge:
8 dc = 1"

Instructions
Ch 6, join to form a ring.

Rnd 1 (right side):
Ch 4 (counts as a dc and a ch-1 sp), (dc in ring, ch 1) 11 times; join in 3rd ch of beg ch-4—12 dc.

Rnd 2:
Ch 3 (counts as a dc on this and following rnds), dc in same ch as joining; ch 1, sk next ch-1 sp; * 2 dc in next dc, ch 1, sk next ch-1 sp; rep from * 10 times more; join in 3rd ch of beg ch-3.

Rnd 3:
Ch 3, dc in same ch as joining and in next dc; ch 2, sk next ch-1 sp; * 2 dc in next dc; dc in next dc, ch 2, sk next ch-1 sp; rep from * 10 times more; join in 3rd ch of beg ch-3.

Rnd 4:
Ch 3, 2 dc in next dc; dc in next dc, ch 3, sk next ch-2 sp; * dc in next dc, 2 dc in next dc; dc in next dc, ch 3, sk next ch-2 sp; rep from * 10 times more; join in 3rd ch of beg ch-3.

Rnd 5:
Ch 3, 2 dc in next dc; dc in next 2 dc, ch 3, sk next ch-3 sp; * dc in next dc, 2 dc in next dc; dc in next 2 dc, ch 3, sk next ch-3 sp; rep from * 10 times more; join in 3rd ch of beg ch-3.

Rnd 6:
Sl st in next 2 dc, ch 5 (counts as a dc and a ch-2 sp), dc in same dc as last sl st made; * ch 6, in 3rd dc of next 5-dc group work (dc, ch 2, dc); rep from * 10 times more; ch 6; join in 3rd ch of beg ch-5.

Rnd 7:
Sl st in next ch-2 sp, ch 3, in same sp work (dc, ch 2, 2 dc); * † ch 6, sk next ch-6 sp, in next ch-2 sp work

(dc, ch 2, dc); ch 6, sk next ch-6 sp †; in next ch-2 sp work (2 dc, ch 2, 2 dc); rep from * 10 times more, then rep from † to † once; join in 3rd ch of beg ch-3.

Rnd 8:
Sl st in next dc and in next ch-2 sp, ch 3, in same sp work (2 dc, ch 3, 3 dc)—beg shell made; * † ch 6, sk next ch-6 sp, in next ch-2 sp work (dc, ch 3, dc); ch 6, sk next ch-6 sp †; in next ch-2 sp work (3 dc, ch 3, 3 dc)—shell made; rep from * 4 times more, then rep from † to † once; join in 3rd ch of beg ch-3—6 shells.

Rnd 9:
Sl st in next 2 dc and in next ch-3 sp; beg shell in same sp; * † ch 5, sk next ch-6 sp, 8 dc in next ch-3 sp—base of pineapple made; ch 5, sk next ch-6 sp †; in ch-3 sp of next shell work shell—shell in shell made; rep from * 4 times more, then rep from † to † once; join in 3rd ch of beg ch-3.

Rnd 10:
Sl st in next 2 dc and in next ch-3 sp, beg shell in same sp; * † ch 4, sk next ch-5 sp, dc in next dc, (ch 1, dc in next dc) 7 times; ch 4, sk next ch-5 sp †; shell in next shell; rep from * 4 times more, then rep from † to † once; join in 3rd ch of beg ch-3.

Rnd 11:
Sl st in next 2 dc and in next ch-3 sp, beg shell in same sp; * † ch 3, sk next ch-4 sp, 3 dc in each of next 7 ch-1 sps; ch 3, sk next ch-4 sp †; shell in next shell; rep from * 4 times more, then rep from † to † once; join in 3rd ch of beg ch-3.

Rnd 12:
Sl st in next 2 dc and in next ch-3 sp, beg shell in same sp; * † ch 3, sk next ch-3 sp, keeping last lp of each trc on hook, trc in next 3 dc, YO and draw through all 4 lps on hook—cluster made; ch 4, (cluster over next 3 dc, ch 4) 5 times; cluster over next 3 dc; ch 3, sk next ch-3 sp †; shell in next shell; rep from * 4 times more, then rep from † to † once; join in 3rd ch of beg ch-3.

Rnd 13:
Sl st in next 2 dc and in next ch-3 sp, beg shell in same sp; ch 3, 3 dc in same sp—beg double shell made; * † ch 3, sk next ch-3 sp, sc in next cluster, (3 sc in next ch-4 sp, sc in next cluster) 6 times; ch 3, sk next ch-3 sp †; shell in next shell; ch 3, 3 dc in same sp—double shell made; rep from * 4 times more, then rep from † to † once; join in 3rd ch of beg ch-3.

Rnd 14:
Sl st in next 2 dc and in next ch-3 sp, beg shell in same sp; * † ch 5, shell in next ch-3 sp; ch 3, sk next ch-3 sp, sc in next sc, (ch 4, sk next 3 sc, sc in next sc) 6 times; ch 3, sk next ch-3 sp †; shell in next ch-3 sp; rep from * 4 times more, then rep from † to † once; join in 3rd ch of beg ch-3.

Rnd 15:
Sl st in next 2 dc and in next ch-3 sp, beg shell in same sp; * † ch 3, sk next 2 chs of next ch-5 sp, shell in next ch; ch 3, shell in next shell; ch 3, sk next ch-3 sp, sc in next ch-4 sp, (ch 4, sc in next ch-4 sp) 5 times; ch 3, sk next ch-3 sp †; shell in next shell; rep from * 4 times more, then rep from † to † once; join in 3rd ch of beg ch-3.

Rnd 16:
Sl st in next 2 dc and in next ch-3 sp, beg shell in same sp; * † ch 5, sk next ch-3 sp, double shell in next shell; ch 5, sk next ch-3 sp, shell in next shell; ch 3, sk next ch-3 sp, sc in next ch-4 sp, (ch 4, sc in next ch-4 sp) 4 times; ch 3, sk next ch-3 sp †; shell in next shell; rep from * 4 times more, then rep from † to † once; join in 3rd ch of beg ch-3.

Rnd 17:
Sl st in next 2 dc and in next ch-3 sp, beg shell in same sp; * † ch 5, sk next ch-5 sp, shell in next sp; ch 5, shell in next ch-3 sp; ch 5, sk next ch-5 sp, shell in next shell; ch 3, sk next ch-3 sp, sc in next ch-4 sp, (ch 4, sc in next ch-4 sp) 3 times; ch 3, sk next ch-3 sp †; shell in next shell; rep from * 4 times more, then rep from † to † once; join in 3rd ch of beg ch-3.

Rnd 18:
Sl st in next 2 dc and in next ch-3 sp, beg shell in same sp; * † ch 5, sk next ch-5 sp, shell in next shell; ch 3, sk next 2 chs of next ch-5 sp, 5 dc in next ch; ch 3, shell in next shell; ch 5, sk next ch-5 sp, shell in next shell; ch 3, sk next ch-3 sp, sc in next ch-4 sp (ch 4, sc in next ch-4 sp) twice; ch 3, sk next ch-3 sp †; shell in next shell; rep from * 4 times more, then rep from † to † once; join in 3rd ch of beg ch-3.

Rnd 19:
Sl st in next 2 dc and in next ch-3 sp, beg shell in same sp; * † ch 5, sk next ch-5 sp, shell in next shell; ch 3, sk next ch-3 sp, 2 dc in next dc; (ch 1, 2 dc in next dc) 4 times; ch 3, sk next ch-3 sp, shell in next shell; ch 5, sk next ch-5 sp, shell in next shell; ch 3, sk next ch-3 sp, sc in next ch-4 sp, ch 4, sc in next ch-4 sp, ch 3, sk next ch-3 sp †; shell in next shell; rep from * 4 times more, then rep from † to † once; join in 3rd ch of beg ch-3.

Rnd 20:
Sl st in next 2 dc and in next ch-3 sp, beg shell in same sp; * † ch 5, sk next ch-5 sp, shell in next shell; ch 3, sk next ch-3 sp, 2 dc in next dc; dc in next dc; †† ch 1, sk next ch-1 sp, 2 dc in next dc; dc in next dc ††; rep from †† to †† 3 times more; ch 3, sk next ch-3 sp, shell in next shell; ch 5, sk next ch-5 sp, shell in next shell; ch 3, sk next ch-3 sp, sc in next ch-4 sp, ch 3, sk next ch-3 sp †; shell in next shell; rep from * 4 times more, then rep from † to † once; join in 3rd ch of beg ch-3.

Rnd 21:
Sl st in next 2 dc and in next ch-3 sp, beg shell in same sp; * † ch 5, sk next ch-5 sp, shell in next shell; ch 3, sk next ch-3 sp, dc in next dc, 2 dc in next dc; dc in next dc; †† ch 1, sk next ch-1 sp, dc in next dc, 2 dc in next dc; dc in next dc ††; rep from †† to †† 3 times more; ch 3 sk next ch-3 sp, shell in next shell; ch 5, sk next ch-5 sp, shell in next shell; sk next 2 ch-3 sps †; shell in next shell; rep from * 4 times more, then rep from † to † once; join in 3rd ch of beg ch-3.

Rnd 22:
Sl st in next 2 dc and in next ch-3 sp, beg shell in same sp; * † ch 5, sk next ch-5 sp, shell in next shell; ch 4, sk next ch-3 sp, dc in next 4 dc; (ch 2, sk next ch-1 sp, dc in next 4 dc) 4 times; ch 4, sk next ch-3 sp, shell in next shell; ch 5, sk next ch-5 sp †; shell in each of next 2 shells; rep from * 4 times more, then rep from † to † once; shell in next shell; join in 3rd ch of beg ch-3.

Rnd 23:
Sl st in next 2 dc and in next ch-3 sp, ch 1, sc in same sp; * † ch 5, sk next ch-5 sp, shell in next shell; ch 5, sk next ch-4 sp, keeping last lp of each dc on hook, dc in next 4 dc; YO and draw through all 5 lps on hook—dc cluster made; (ch 5, sk next ch-1 sp, dc cluster over next 4 dc) 4 times; ch 5, sk next ch-4 sp, shell in next shell; ch 5, sk next ch-5 sp, sc in ch-3 sp of next shell, ch 7 †; sc in ch-3 sp of next shell; rep from * 4 times more, then rep from † to † once; join in first sc.

Rnd 24:
Ch 1, sc in same sc; * † 4 sc in next ch-5 sp; sc in next 3 dc, 3 sc in next ch-3 sp; sc in next 3 dc; †† 4 sc in next ch-5 sp, in next dc cluster work (sc, ch 4, sc)††; rep from †† to †† 4 times more; 4 sc in next ch-5 sp; sc in next 3 dc, 3 sc in next ch-3 sp; sc in next 3 dc, 4 sc in next ch-5 sp; sc in next sc, 6 sc in next ch-5 sp †; sc in next sc; rep from * 4 times more, then rep from † to † once; join in first sc.
Finish off and weave in ends.

Abbreviations and Symbols

beg ....begin(ning)
ch(s) .... chain(s)
dc..double crochet(s)
dec.. decrease(-ing)
gm(s).. gram(s)
hdc .... half double crochet(s)
lp(s) .... loop(s)
oz...ounce(s)
patt .... pattern
prev .... previous
rem... remain(ing)
rep ....repeat(ing)
sc .... single crochet(s)
sl st(s) .... slip stitch(es)
sp(s) .... space(s)
st(s) .... stitch(es)
tog ....together
trc ....triple crochet(s)
yd(s) .... yard(s)
YO .... yarn over

* An asterisk is used to mark the beginning of a portion of instructions to be worked more than once; thus, "rep from * twice more" means after working the instructions once, repeat the instructions following the asterisk twice more (3 times in all).

† The dagger identifies a portion of instructions that will be repeated again later in the same row or round.

— The number after a long dash at the end of a row or round indicates the number of stitches you should have when the row or round has been completed. The long dash can also be used to indicate a completed stitch such as a decrease, a shell or a cluster.

() Parentheses are used to enclose instructions that should be worked the exact number of times specified immediately following the parentheses, such as "(2 sc in next dc, sc in next dc) twice." They are also used to set off and clarify a group of stitches that are to be worked all into the same space or stitch, such as "in next corner sp work (2 dc, ch 1, 2 dc)."

[] Brackets and () parentheses are used to provide additional information to clarify instructions.

Join—join with a sl st unless otherwise specified.

The patterns in this book are written using United States terminology. Terms that have different English equivalents are noted below.

United States	English
single crochet (sc)	double crochet (dc)
half double crochet (hdc)	half treble (htr)
double crochet (dc)	treble (tr)
triple crochet (trc)	double treble (dtr)
skip (sk)	miss
slip stitch (sl st)	slip stitch (ss) or single crochet
gauge	tension
yarn over (YO)	yarn over hook (YOH)

How to Check Gauge

A correct stitch gauge is very important. Please take the time to work a stitch gauge swatch about 4" x 4". Measure the swatch. If the number of stitches and rows are fewer than indicated under "Gauge" in the pattern, your hook is too large. Try another swatch with a smaller size hook. If the number of stitches and rows are more than indicated under "Gauge" in the pattern, your hook is too small. Try another swatch with a larger size hook.

Metric Conversion Charts

INCHES INTO MILLIMETERS & CENTIMETERS (Rounded off slightly)

inches	mm	cm	inches	cm	inches	cm	inches	cm
1/8	3		5	12.5	21	53.5	38	96.5
1/4	6		5 1/2	14	22	56	39	99
3/8	10	1	6	15	23	58.5	40	101.5
1/2	13	1.3	7	18	24	61	41	104
5/8	15	1.5	8	20.5	25	63.5	42	106.5
3/4	20	2	9	23	26	66	43	109
7/8	22	2.2	10	25.5	27	68.5	44	112
1	25	2.5	11	28	28	71	45	114.5
1 1/4	32	3.2	12	30.5	29	73.5	46	117
1 1/2	38	3.8	13	33	30	76	47	119.5
1 3/4	45	4.5	14	35.5	31	79	48	122
2	50	5	15	38	32	81.5	49	124.5
2 1/2	65	6.5	16	40.5	33	84	50	127
3	75	7.5	17	43	34	86.5		
3 1/2	90	9	18	46	35	89		
4	100	10	19	48.5	36	91.5		
4 1/2	115	11.5	20	51	37	94		

CROCHET HOOKS CONVERSION CHART

U.S.	00	0	1	2	3	4	5	6	7	8	9	10	11	12	13	14
Continental-mm	3.50	3.25	2.75	2.25	2.10	2.00	1.90	1.80	1.65	1.50	1.40	1.30	1.10	1.00	0.85	0.75

Skill Levels

BEGINNER

Projects for first-time crocheters using basic stitches. Minimal shaping.

EASY

Projects using yarn with basic stitches, repetitive stitch patterns, simple color changes, and simple shaping and finishing.

INTERMEDIATE

Projects using a variety of techniques, such as basic lace patterns or color patterns, mid-level shaping and finishing.

EXPERIENCED

Projects with intricate stitch patterns, techniques and dimension, such as non-repeating patterns, multi-color techniques, fine threads, small hooks, detailed shaping and refined finishing.

Stitch Guide

Chain—ch:
YO, draw through lp on hook.

Single Crochet—sc:
Insert hook in st, YO and draw through, YO and draw through both lps on hook.

Reverse Single Crochet—Reverse sc:
Work from left to right, insert hook in sp or st indicated (**a**), draw lp through sp or st—2 lps on hook (**b**); YO and draw through lps on hook.

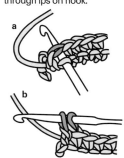

Half Double Crochet—hdc:
YO, insert hook in st, YO, draw through, YO and draw through all 3 lps on hook.

Double Crochet—dc:
YO, insert hook in st, YO, draw through, (YO and draw through 2 lps on hook) twice.

Triple Crochet—trc:
YO twice, insert hook in st, YO, draw through, (YO and draw through 2 lps on hook) 3 times.

Slip Stitch—sl st:
(a) Used for Joinings
Insert hook in indicated st, YO and draw through st and lp on hook.

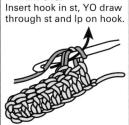

(b) Used for Moving Yarn Over
Insert hook in st, YO draw through st and lp on hook.

Front Loop—FL:
The front loop is the loop toward you at the top of the stitch.

Back Loop—BL:
The back loop is the loop away from you at the top of the stitch.

Post:
The post is the vertical part of the stitch.

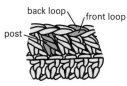

Overcast Stitch is worked loosely to join crochet pieces.

American School of Needlework®
excellence in instruction

2420 Grand Avenue, Suite H
Vista, CA 92081-7827
ASNpub.com

©2004 American School of Needlework, Inc.
The full line of ASN products is carried by Annie's Attic catalog.
TOLL-FREE ORDER LINE or to request a free catalog **(800) 582-6643**

Visit AnniesAttic.com.

Customer Service (800) 282-6643, fax (800) 882-6643